Through the Eyes of Your Ancestors

Through the Eyes

of Your Ancestors

Maureen A. Taylor

Houghton Mifflin Company Boston 1999

The text of this book is set in 12.75-point Palatino.

Library of Congress Cataloging-in-Publication Data

Taylor, Maureen, 1955 –
Through the eyes of your ancestors / Maureen Taylor.
p.   cm.
Includes bibliographical references.
Summary: Discusses genealogy, the study of one's family,
examining how such an interest develops, how to get started,
how to use family stories and keepsakes, where to get help,
and the positive effects of such study.
RNF ISBN 0-395-86980-3   PAP ISBN 0-395-86982-X
1. Genealogy — Juvenile literature.   [1. Genealogy.]
I. Title   CS15.5.T39   1999
929'.1 — dc21   98-8776   CIP   AC

Manufactured in the United States of America
CRW 10 9 8 7 6 5 4 3 2 1

Acknowledgments

This book would not have been possible without the support of
several friends and colleagues who offered encouragement along
the way, including Lynn Betlock, Jane Schwerdtfeger, Leslie Schuster,
D. Brenton Simons, and especially Henry Hoff. The patient staff
of the Westwood Public Library retrieved countless books during
the preparation of this one. Special thanks are due to my family for
making me believe this book was possible.

To my children,
James and Sarah, who will have their own stories to tell,
and to Gramma Eliza for sharing her memories.

Family history is about exploring the past. What were your parents' and grandparents' lives like when they were your age?

Table of Contents

Families are created by a series of events.

1. Our Families

At some point in their lives, most people want to learn more about their families. This interest can start with a simple question and become a lifelong pursuit.

Angela asked her parents about their childhoods and how they met. "My parents encouraged me to talk to other members of my family. It was amazing to find out what their lives were like at my age."

According to Michael, his interest in genealogy began when he found a history of his family. "It contained the names and dates of my ancestors back to the colonial days. I read it and was fascinated by the fact that these people were relatives. They actually participated in events I was studying in school. It seemed unbeliev-able to me that all of these people had at some point been my age."

Michael and Angela became family historians. They began to collect not only the facts about their ancestors but their history as well. Some people compile journals about their families; others express their history in artistic ways. By looking into the past, a family historian can sometimes glimpse the future. Will an individual become a farmer like her grandparents or follow in her parents' footsteps? By researching our family's history, we discover ourselves through our relatives.

Genealogy is the study of one's family. It comes from two Greek words that mean "family" and "science." Genealogy has been pursued by virtually all cultures around the world. Prior to written records, genealogy consisted of oral traditions. In sixth-century Japan, family history combined mythology and genealogy. Written or printed genealogies of European royalty first appeared several hundred years ago. Queen Elizabeth II and millions of other people can trace their ancestry in some of these genealogies back to the year 500!

For centuries in Europe, genealogy focused on members of royal families. The lineage or line of direct descent determined who would ascend to the throne. Formal record keeping and genealogy for the common man began at different times depending on the culture or country. In Yorkshire, England, some land records exist for tenants from the thirteenth century.

Today, many people think of their family history and genealogy as their personal detective story. One's story can either begin with an immigrant ancestor and progress in time, or it can begin in the present and work backward. A genealogy is often a list of family members; a family

You can't learn about family origins simply by looking at a person's face or learning his or her name — only research will help you uncover the past.

history can be more of a narrative. A family history can include the stories, photographs, and keepsakes of those individuals.

A family is a group of people related by birth, marriage, or events. A family is as unique as a person is. Families have always been full of interesting variations and stories. Mothers, fathers, children, cousins, uncles, aunts, and grandparents are part of an extended kinship group. Blended families may include birthparents, adoptive parents, stepparents, and stepchildren. A genealogy or family history is a reflection of one's family. It can help people understand the influences that make them who they are.

One can include friends and even pets in a family history. Some individuals write novels based on their genealogy. Alex Haley's fictionalized account of his family in his book *Roots* inspired many people to seek out the origins of their families. He brought genealogy to life by including oral traditions about African origins and some facts of his ancestry that he discov-

An interest in family history often starts with a series of questions, such as how members of your family met.

ered through research. We can be as creative as we wish with the compilation of our family history.

In 1878, twelve-year-old Bertie L.

3

Martin kept a journal of the time he spent living on his grandfather's farm. He recorded his personal feelings and farm experiences. Bertie also wrote a short genealogy based on the stories his grandparents told him. He traced three generations of his family in his diary. He started with the earliest ancestor he knew of and ended with himself. He included the names of ancestors important to his sense of family history. It was a simple listing of names and dates, but it was his first

There have always been many different kinds of families. Think about the individuals who are part of your family.

attempt to chronicle his family.

Jennifer's history includes not only information about the members of her household, but the story of her adoption and her birthparents as well. Her parents maintained an adoption scrapbook of photographs, letters, and playthings, so she decided to study both of her families. Andrew is a member of a large extended family that immigrated to the United States over a long period of time. He chose to focus on how his family arrived in America and the traditions they brought with them. James is from a family that can trace its ancestry back to the American Revolution, and he included in his genealogy a description of an ancestor who met George Washington.

Family history is an adventure because you never know what will be uncovered. Research into a family's history usually reveals new information, such as the fact that a set of ancestors traveled across the country in search of gold or that an ancestor was adopted. A person may learn that her family's ethnic heritage is more diverse than she thought. A name that sounds English may actually be a translation from another language. A researcher may discover that his or her ancestors came from many different countries. If a person's ancestry is not Native American, his or her family originally came to the United States from another country. It is important to remember that people from all racial and ethnic groups settled in the United States.

In order to reveal the history of a family, one needs to ask relatives and to use libraries to do research. Genealogy is an exciting undertaking that brings history and ancestors to life. This book is full of stories of people who have had fun researching their families, and who have learned more about themselves in the process.

Focus on coats of arms

There are books of coats of arms in most libraries and bookstores, but individuals can use a coat of arms or heraldic emblem only if they are a direct descendant of the person for whom it was designed.

Heraldry developed in the early Middle Ages as a way to identify soldiers on the battlefield, because men in full armor were unrecognizable. The shield displayed the coat of arms on the battlefield. No two men were supposed to wear the same coat of arms. Women could use their fathers' arms. When a woman married, that design became part of her husband's shield design.

There are two groups in the United States that recognize new coats of arms. The New England Historic Genealogical Society in Boston has a Committee on Heraldry that accepts claims for arms submitted by individuals. The American College of Heraldry in Maryland, founded in 1972, will issue arms for individuals and corporations. In order to correctly use a coat of arms, one needs to prove that he or she is a direct descendant of the person to whom it belonged.

Older relatives can be an excellent resource for information and stories. Are stories being passed on in your family?

2. Family Stories and Keepsakes

An individual can start a genealogy by selecting a relative with whom she feels comfortable and arranging a time for an interview. A good opportunity to informally ask relatives questions about the family is at a special event or holiday. These occasions are an opportunity to identify the people with the best memories and those most willing to discuss family matters. The material one accumulates in this way provides a background for more personal interviews. After a family party, Margaret knew that her great-aunt would be an excellent resource for family lore. Even though her aunt initially refused to talk with her, Margaret persisted.

"After several years of asking, my great-aunt finally decided that I could interview her for my family history. She confessed that she had been reluctant to speak with me because she felt that some family information was confidential and should be forgotten! But since she had just celebrated her ninetieth birthday, she could now tell me about people and events that had happened many years ago." Margaret spent a great deal of time collecting facts on her mother's family, but she wanted to add thorough accuracy to the family biographies. By seeking out her oldest relative, she hoped to add life and detail to her genealogy. Her great-aunt helped her fill in the blanks about family members she had never met. After the interview, Margaret tried hard to verify through research what her great-aunt told her.

Just as Margaret's great-aunt expressed an unwillingness to talk with her, members of your own family may not want to discuss certain things. Do not be surprised when a relative avoids discussing an event or person by saying "He didn't turn out well" or "You don't want to know about that." All families have stories that they would prefer not to appear in a genealogy. Reluctance can perhaps be overcome with sensitivity and persistence. If a family member refuses to discuss something, try to learn the facts through investigation or talk with a different relative.

Many families maintain an oral tradition about dramatic or humorous events. In one family, a pioneer ancestor saved a town from wolves by tracking them in a snowstorm. His adventures became family legend based on fact but exaggerated for the sake of a good story. One woman recalled that her parents caught her using a grindstone to wear down the soles of her shoes so that she could get new ones.

Margaret prepared for her visit by making a list of questions. It is best to start with simple questions and let a relative expand on his memories. Gentle remind-

Encourage storytelling by asking about humorous or dramatic events.

ers will guide a relative back to the question, since a query may lead him to reminisce about events not directly related to the topic.

Potential questions to ask a family member

- Who were your brothers and sisters?
- What do you remember about your grandparents?
- Where have you lived?
- How did your family celebrate holidays?
- What did you imagine your life would be like?
- What are your fondest childhood memories?

For relatives who live too far away to visit, create a form letter with blanks for them to fill in, in addition to a list of general questions. Your father was _____. He was born on _____ in _____. Try to keep questions short to encourage the person to return the answers. Remember that the person answering the questionnaire may not be interested in family genealogy.

Some ethnic groups maintain their family genealogy as an oral tradition. The family or tribal elders can recount the story of their family in detail for several generations.

Interview individuals about their lives — try to get more information than their names and their dates of births, marriages, and deaths.

Artifacts are often passed down from generation to generation. Look around your house for items that can be conversation starters.

In other families, family artifacts are important. Mary and Mark are siblings who are researching different parts of their family through keepsakes. Mark inherited heirlooms from his stepfather's family. Along with the pieces of furniture that he received, he found letters and deeds from family members. He set out to locate information on these individuals by following the clues in the documents and by contacting living relatives.

Mary remembered her visits to her grandparents. "They lived in a house built by an ancestor in 1809. On each of my visits my grandmother would show me things that had special meaning for her. She was very proud of a set of three samplers that hung in the living room. Each one commemorated a golden wedding anniversary and was stitched by a child of the couple depicted in the sampler. Three generations of the family were represented in that room. The marriages of my grandparents, great-grandparents, and great-great-grandparents were immortalized in thread."

Photographs, jewelry, quilts, baby toys, and even recipes are often passed from generation to generation. In the photographs, one might find a picture of someone holding the doll that is now owned by someone in the current generation. One woman owns her great-grandmother's cookbook, complete with handwritten notations. Articles of furniture owned by an ancestor may still be in the family. Mary learned that her grandfather slept in the same bed in which he was born. Her grandmother would also show her a Bible that contained handwritten notes of the birth, marriages, and deaths in the family.

An artifact can be any item that once belonged to another family member. Do not despair if a family does not have any heirlooms. Families often forget boxes stored in the attic, basement, garage, or barn. When visiting relatives, ask if they own anything that brings back special memories. In one family, a piece of china recalls the courtship and marriage of a couple; in another a portrait of an ancestor has special meaning. While the artifacts and heirlooms are significant, the family stories will bring them to life.

An item that now belongs to you may once have belonged to another family member.

Items that will guide your research

- photographs (albums, movies, videos)
- scrapbooks
- family Bibles
- announcements and invitations
- letters and diaries
- furniture

- jewelry
- silver
- souvenirs

Focus on photographs

Sometimes researchers discover a box of photographs of the family. They have no idea how to organize and care for them or even who all of the people are. Here are a few tips to help organize them.

1. Wear clean white cotton gloves from the hardware store when handling the photos. If gloves are not available, hold the photos by the edges.

2. Lay them out on a clean, flat surface and look for identifying physical characteristics. Perhaps an ancestor has a scar, a style of dressing, or other distinguishing features that will help you group the images.

3. Try to find out how old the photos are by dating the style of clothing and the type of photograph, or through the name of the photographer that may appear on the image. Most public libraries have cos-tume encyclopedias in their collections.

4. Show the photos to as many relatives as possible. Someone else in the family may recognize the people in them.

5. Remember to handle the photos with care. Try to avoid touching the images directly.

These types of photographs are commonly found in family collections:

Daguerreotype (1839–1860s). This one-of-a-kind image on metal resembles a mirror. In order to see the image try different angles until it is clearly seen. It is usually found in a case.
Ambrotype (1850s–1890s). This is a one-of-a-kind image on glass. It is usually found in a case.
Carte de visite (1850s–1890s). A small photograph mounted on a card. The name of the photographer usually appears on the back of the card.
Ferreotype or tin type (1850s–1920s). A photograph on metal that has a black back.
Cabinet card (1885–1920). A photograph

mounted on a card larger than a carte de visite. The photographer's name appears on the front of the card beneath the image.

Snapshots (1885–present). The first snapshot camera was manufactured by Kodak. The film was returned to the factory for developing. Their slogan was, "You press the button, and we do the rest." Color candid photography first appeared in the 1920s.

Polaroid (1948–present). These photographs develop outside the camera. They are known as instant photographs because they develop while a person watches.

Look for information about your family in town historical societies.

3. Getting Started

"When I was a child, my family moved eight or nine times, and I remember feeling no connection with extended family members," recalled Lynn. "Several generations of my family, including my parents, were from a small town in Minnesota called Little Falls. Whenever I visited my grandparents, they would tell me stories about my family and their lives in Little Falls. On one particular visit, my grandparents took me to the Morrison County Museum and showed me files on my family. I was amazed that a museum would have information on my relatives! The archives contained a history of how my family came to America. I immediately went home and ordered forms to keep track of my gene-alogy, just like the museum had." Lynn also began corresponding with an aunt in California about the family and discovered that they shared a common interest in genealogy. From the files at the museum, the stories her grandparents told, and the material her aunt had collected, Lynn learned a great deal about her background. Genealogy helped Lynn reconnect with her family.

Not everyone can locate his or her family in an archive. The idea of researching a family seems complicated and overwhelming at first. If one breaks the process down into smaller steps, that hesitation may turn into an excitement about discovering the unknown. There are five basic steps in a family history project:

choosing equipment; creating a record-keeping strategy; identifying what you know and do not know; undertaking the research; and compiling the results. Genealogy does not seem so overwhelming if it is done a step at a time.

The most helpful supplies to have for your research are a notebook and pencil combined with a generous amount of curiosity. With these, you can create the forms and charts that will help organize the research. Other optional equipment includes a camera, tape recorder, computer, or video camera. The camera is handy for photographing relatives, artifacts, and gravestones. The tape recorder and video camera are helpful when you interview individuals. A computer can connect a researcher with the world of genealogy via the Internet or help a person create a format for the material. Genealogy is a hobby that can be expensive or inexpensive, depending on the resources available to the researcher. Most people start armed only with a simple piece of paper and a writing implement.

Helpful tools

- pencil or pen
- notebook
- camera (optional)
- tape recorder (optional)
- video camera (optional)
- computer (optional)

The next step is to set up a record-keeping system in order to report the material obtained from individuals and other research. The basis of all good investigations is the preliminary planning, which helps an individual identify the questions that need answers.

One way that researchers record their findings and plan their study is through the use of forms and charts. There are several different types of forms. The most popular forms are the pedigree chart, the family group sheet, and the research log. The pedigree chart is the most widely available because it is simple to use. A standard chart has four or five generations per page with space to record birth, death,

Pedigree Chart

Chart Number _____

Number 1 on this chart is the same as
Number _____ on
Chart Number _____

YOUR GREAT GRANDFATHER
8. Born:
Place:
Married:
Place:
Died:
Place:

YOUR GRANDFATHER
4. Born:
Place:
Married:
Place:
Died:
Place:

YOUR GREAT GRANDMOTHER
9. Born:
Place:
Died:
Place

YOUR FATHER
2. Born:
Place:
Married:
Place:
Died:
Place:

YOUR GREAT GRAND FATHER
10. Born:
Place:
Married:
Place:
Died:
Place:

YOUR GRANDMOTHER
5. Born:
Place:
Died:
Place

YOUR GREAT GRANDMOTHER
11. Born:
Place:
Died:
Place

YOU
1. Born:
Place:
Married:
Place:

YOUR GREAT GRANDFATHER
12. Born:
Place:
Married:
Place:
Died:
Place:

YOUR GRANDFATHER
6. Born:
Place:
Married:
Place:
Died:
Place:

YOUR GREAT GRANDMOTHER
13. Born:
Place:
Died:
Place

YOUR MOTHER
3. Born:
Place:
Died:
Place

YOUR GREAT GRAND FATHER
14. Born:
Place:
Married:
Place:
Died:
Place:

YOUR GRANDMOTHER
7. Born:
Place:
Died:
Place

YOUR GREAT GRANDMOTHER
15. Born:
Place:
Died:
Place

and marriage data on each person. At least four generations of both a mother's side of the family (maternal) and a father's side of the family (paternal) fit on the first sheet. More sheets can be added as needed. You can start with yourself and work backward, creating an outline of your family. Assign a number to each person on the chart in order to keep track of him or her. In the standard method, the researcher is number 1, her parents are 2 and 3, and her grandparents are 4 through 8. Every generation doubles the number of direct ancestors. By the tenth generation, there are at least 512 ancestors. This does not include siblings.

The second type of form, the family group sheet, helps to track information on each individual family. A person should create a family group sheet for each couple on the pedigree chart. The form provides a good checklist of information to collect, including material on siblings. It is a good place to footnote data.

Every time a person contacts someone or looks at a document, he should write down the location of the information. It is very important to record sources. A genealogist once waited six months for a librarian to return from a leave of absence in hope that she would recall the source of a particular page. Unfortunately the librarian was unable to identify the source after such a long time. It is very important to keep track of research in case it needs to be reviewed at a later time. A complete reference includes the name of the author, book title, place of publication, publisher, date of publication, and page numbers. A good way to keep a record of a correct citation is to photocopy the title page. The first page of a book usually lists the author and title.

Early in your research, it is a good idea to make a checklist of information that you need to verify. A log helps to plan a strategy. You should create a separate log for each ancestor. Describe the documents that you hope to find. A simple log lists documents to locate, where to find them, and the data that they might provide. An accurate log prevents duplication and helps individuals plan efficient research trips.

Family Group Sheet

Husband's Full Name:_____

Date	Day/Month/Year	Town/County/State	Additional Info.	Sources
Birth				
Marriage				
Death				
Burial				

Places of Residence:	Occupation:

Military Record:	Religion:	Social Security #:

Other Wives:

Additional Info. (name changes, adoption, divorce)

His Father:	His Mother:

Wife's Full Maiden Name:_____

Date	Day/Month/Year	Town/County/State	Additional Info.	Sources
Birth				
Death				
Burial				

Places of Residence:	Occupation:

Military Record:	Religion:	Social Security #:

Other Husbands:

Additional Info. (name changes, adoption, divorce)

Her Father:	Her Mother:

Children (In birth order)	Sex	Birth (date and place)	Marriage (date and place)	Death (date and place)	Source

Genealogy Research Log

Ancestor's Name HARRY MANSFIELD WILSON			Chart Number /	
Information Needed DATE OF BIRTH / PARENTS NAMES			Location	

Date of Search	Location/ Call No.	Source	Comments	Document Number
6/26/ 1995	PAWTUCKET CITY HALL	DEATH RECORDS 1910	vol. 4 page 302	
6/27/1995	NEHGS MICROTEXT DEPT.	INDEX TO MASSACHUSETTS VITAL RECORDS 1841 –	NOT FOUND	

Some people prefer to use a computer to help them organize their family history. Software choices range from a simple word-processing program to a genealogical software package. Write down the tasks you want your program to perform and then consult reviews of the software before final purchase. Certain companies will send a demo version you can try out.

Computer programs that will assist you

Master Genealogist. This program includes a research log and a date calculator. It has the ability to incorporate photographs and sound recordings.

Personal Ancestry File. Developed by the Church of Jesus Christ of Latter-day Saints, this program is available in a DOS version or for the Macintosh. You can download information from the Family Search Program (available at Family History Centers) into this program.

Family Tree Maker. This is a user-friendly program that allows you to incorporate material retrieved from the *Family Tree Maker* set of informational CD-ROMs.

Reunion. This was one of the first programs that could print graphic tree charts with photographs. This program accepts information on adoptions and nontraditional families.

You may also want to create a family time line in order to place your ancestors in a historical context. First, write down the important dates in U.S. history, such as the Civil War. Next, record the significant dates for a family, such as year of immigration and dates of birth, marriage, and death. Write the names of the people next to the events. Look for instances in which historical events intersect with family history. By identifying historical events, a researcher can try to locate documents to fill in additional material. For instance, if several members of a family lived at the time of the Civil War, a researcher should attempt to locate military records for those individuals. Time-lines help to identify patterns that repeat in each generation, such as military service or settlement.

After you choose the equipment, select the forms, and list the people to locate, the next step is to investigate the individuals on the family group sheets and logs. There are many different types of documents that you will encounter.

Try to find vital records: birth, marriage, and death records. These can contain an ancestor's full name, her parents'

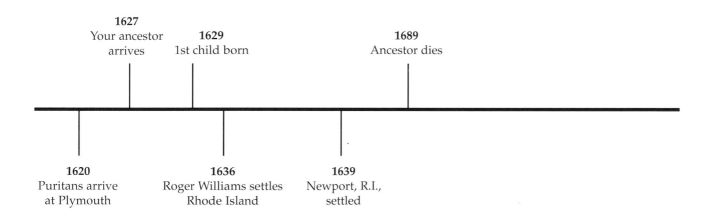

| 1627 Your ancestor arrives | 1629 1st child born | 1689 Ancestor dies |

1620 Puritans arrive at Plymouth

1636 Roger Williams settles Rhode Island

1639 Newport, R.I., settled

Birth and marriage records are a good source of family information.

names, and places of birth. Records can often be found in town and state government offices. Remember that official registrations of births, marriages, and deaths were not kept in most states until the mid-nineteenth century. Several states did not begin keeping vital statistics until the early twentieth century!

Religious records are another good resource for locating ancestors. Religion was an important part of our ancestors' lives. Many denominations kept records of their members. Baptismal and marriage records, for instance, will provide the names of witnesses who may also be relatives. Burial records may furnish the name of the cemetery where you can go to examine gravestones.

Religious groups created different kinds of registers for their members, and some are more complete than others. Many families changed religious affiliations. It may be a surprise to discover that ancestors attended several different churches in their lifetime.

Even if you can find documentation of the births, marriages, and deaths of ancestors, it is a good idea to look for additional records to verify what was found. The United States takes a census every ten years. The early censuses that were taken from 1790 to 1840 recorded only the name of the head of the household and the number of people living in the household. In 1850, census-takers began to record the names and ages of everyone in the household. Early-twentieth-century census records include the year of immigration and year of birth. The types of documents available depend on where and when an ancestor lived.

Types of records

Vital records: Birth, death, and marriage records

Land records: Documents relating to the buying and selling of land

Probate records: Wills, adoptions, and guardianships

Court records: Legal material consisting of divorces and civil and criminal cases

Church records: Baptisms, marriages, burial records, and school reports

Cemetery records: Burial records

Naturalizations: Citizenship papers

Passenger lists: A list of the individuals on a particular ship and day; a record of border crossings

Newspapers: Contain personal notices, advertisements, and news

City directories: A listing of individuals and businesses in a community

Focus on calendars

As you fill out a pedigree chart, be sure to include the dates of births, marriages, and deaths. This seems like an easy task, but it is not always the case. Time period and religious affiliation influenced the style of recording dates. When we look at a calendar, it's difficult to imagine how to record the days in any other way; however, approximately forty different calendars are used around the world today. The three most commonly followed calendars are the Gregorian calendar and two religious calendars, the Islamic and the Hebrew.

Calendars fall into three categories: solar, which is based on the sun; lunar, which is based on the phases of the moon; and unisolar, based on both. The Gregorian calendar is solar; the Islamic calendar is lunar; and the Hebrew calendar is unisolar. In all three systems, the length of a day is the amount of time it takes for the earth to make one complete turn on its axis. A month refers to the time the moon takes to complete a full cycle of its phases.

First communion and other religious records can be helpful to a genealogist.

A year is the time it takes the earth to rotate around the sun. Man created the concept of hours and weeks to add more order to the calendar. Constantine I introduced the seven-day week in the fourth century.

The calendar we use today evolved from the Roman or Julian calendar , which was a lunar calendar of only ten months. Because this calendar did not accurately reflect the number of days in a year, it was amended.

The most recent changes have been made to the Gregorian calendar. Many countries switched to the Gregorian calendar in 1587, but some Protestant countries, including England and the American colonies, did not adopt this calendar until 1752. Russia and Greece did not adopt the Gregorian calendar until the twentieth century. If a date is followed by an O.S. or an N.S., this refers to the old or new calendar. (O.S. means old-style; N.S. means new-style.) Dates recorded with a slash through the middle of the year, for example, 1720/21, also refer to this difference.

In Quaker records (and in the Julian calendar until 1752), the first month of the year is March, not January. For example, an event recorded as the third month refers to May, not March.

Date notations can confuse even the most experienced genealogist, so do be careful when transcribing dates from documents.

Immigrants sometimes changed their names by shortening or Anglicizing them.

4. What Does That Mean?

Alex spent a lot of time listening to his relatives reminisce about their lives. He particularly recalls his grandfather's story of how he immigrated to America. "My grandfather used to tell me that he had a different name before he immigrated. Having a lively imagination, I was sure that my grandfather was in some kind of trouble. He couldn't tell me why it was changed, only that it had happened." Alex's grandfather recalled that he arrived at Ellis Island, told the immigration official his surname, and then suddenly had a new one. Alex later learned that his grandfather thought that if the immigration officer couldn't understand the name, he assigned a new one. As Alex's grandfather met other immigrants, he heard similar stories. Some of his grandfather's friends later changed their names so that they could more easily find employment and avoid discrimination. In actuality, immigration officials changed very few names because they were working from a list of passengers created at the port of departure. Many immigrants changed their names before leaving their homelands by shortening them by a syllable or two.

"Genealogy also taught me not to assume anything. As I listened to my family talk, I realized that their lives were very different from my own. My aunt used to talk about when she was a 'typewriter.' She explained that she was a secretary but that she was called a typewriter because she used one. She helped me understand that the meanings of words change over time and that some become extinct. It was exciting to learn about language and the meanings of words and names."

Genealogy makes us aware of the passage of time. Some documents list occupations that no longer exist, names

Genealogy teaches us about how words and meanings evolve over time. Women clerks were called typewriters.

that are spelled differently, and ancestors who have unusual names. Word usage was also different. When reading a document written by or for an ancestor, someone may think they know the meaning of a word, but it does not fit the context of the sentence or document. Regional and ethnic variations exist for even the most common words. For instance, the word "dinner" was first used in a book in 1622 as referring to a meal, but by 1867 it specifically designated the noon meal. In the twentieth century, dinner could mean the midday or the evening meal. Some words actually come to mean the opposite of their original usage. The word "awesome" used to mean full of awe or dreadful, but today it refers to something remarkable. Technology and foreign languages bring new words into our language every day.

The ability to spell words or names consistently is a product of education. Most of our ancestors were not as well educated as we are today, and therefore words and names will be spelled in every imaginable way. Children often worked alongside their parents in the fields and factories. Education was a luxury. Most people could write their names, but not everyone could read. If a family immigrated from a non-English-speaking country, the inability to understand English was a barrier to employment and education.

Many of the documents you locate during your research will have words spelled differently due to the lack of formal education. The spelling of names and words will be associated with how your ancestors sounded out those words. Spelling did not become standard until the late nineteenth century.

The spelling and usage of names evolved over centuries. For instance, James Kelley's last name appeared in various ways on different documents. It appeared as Kelley, Kelly, Killey, and O'Killea. When researching a name, think of alternate ways to spell it. If you cannot locate a surname, try to spell it as it sounds in order to find variant spellings. The U.S. government uses a Soundex index system to group names of similar spellings. This system helps researchers locate family members in the census.

Soundex

Use the first letter and the next three consonants of a name to learn the code. Letters that sound alike are not coded, and double letters are coded as a single letter. If there are fewer than three consonants, fill in with zeros.

1: b,f,p,v
2: c,g,j,k,q,s,x,z
3: d,t
4: l
5: m,n
6: r
A,e,i,o,u,h,w, and y are not coded.

For example, the code for Taylor is T-460. The code for Bell is B-400.

A phone book for an area contains an amazing assortment of names. According to the 1990 U.S. census, the most common name is Smith, followed by several other English-sounding names. This is misleading, because only about half of the people with this name are of English descent. There are variations of Smith in many different languages. Li is the most common name in the world, shared by more than 87 million people.

Certain surnames are more prevalent in different areas of the country due to the patterns of settlement of ethnic groups. The Hispanic names Garcia and Martinez are common names in the United States today, but they are most common in the Southwest.

Surnames were developed to help distinguish people as populations grew. In England, common men's names were Henry, William, Robert, John, and Richard. The only way to distinguish them was to add further information to the name, such as John of the Hill, Richard of the Green, or John the Smith. Surnames often fall into four categories: geographic, occupational, family (patronymic), and descriptive. Many families know the ethnic heritage and language of their surname but not the meaning.

A geographic name generally means that the first person to receive it lived near that place. John Hill probably lived near a hill. Other names include Brook and Water. The meaning of a name is not always apparent at first glance; for instance, Kelly can mean hill or grove.

Occupational surnames are also common, such as Smith, from working with metal, wood, or stone. Another example is Taylor. This was a person who worked with cloth. Names ending with "man" can refer to someone who was a servant. Bateman, for instance, may mean servant to Bates.

Similarly, patronymic names, meaning "from the father," often end with "son" (identifying the child of the man). For instance, Robertson means the son of Robert and Peterson means the son of Peter.

Certain names describe physical attributes or characteristics. Strong and Little are obvious, but what about Lyon? It could mean brave as a lion.

Many surnames are derived from occupations.

Top ten surnames in the United States

Smith: an occupational name for a metal, stone, or wood worker

Johnson: a patronymic for the son of John

Williams: a patronymic for the son of William

Brown: a nickname that refers to the color of hair, complexion, or clothing

Jones: a name derived from the son of John

Miller: an occupational name for someone who runs a mill

Davis: the son of David

Wilson: a patronymic for the son of William

Anderson: the son of Andrew

Taylor: an occupational name that usually referred to one who sewed.

Until recently, names passed from father to children and from husband to wife in the United States. Today, a woman can retain her maiden name (the name she was given at birth, generally her father's surname) or join it to her husband's with a hyphen, and she can pass it on to her child.

After the Civil War, African Americans freed from slavery chose names for their families. Slaveholders often separated slave families; therefore, several branches of the same family might use different surnames.

Jewish surnames were not standardized until governments made all citizens register their birth in the 1800s. Until then, many Jewish families changed their last names with every generation to include the father's name and a word meaning "son of."

Adopted children may have a different first and last name from their birth name. Some adoptive parents retain a child's first name to acknowledge her cultural heritage.

Many people who live in the United States have three names: a first, middle, and last name. First names are also known as personal, given, or Christian names.

First names are often passed on from generation to generation.

Parents sometimes name their children after relatives or famous people. In James Kelley's family, a child named James appears in every generation from 1830 to the present.

Trends in first names date back to the first immigrants. Colonial families in New England typically used biblical names, while settlers in Virginia often named their sons after English monarchs. Occasionally, a name commemorated a special event; for example, Oceanus Hopkins was born on the Mayflower in 1620. At other times, it appears, names were given at random. Some of them seem amusing to us today. How about a name like Preserved Fish? He was a prominent merchant in New England, and his name was notorious! Settlers in certain parts of the country created given names for their children much as parents do today, trying to find a name to match the uniqueness of their child. Slaveholders often used Greek and Roman names like Caesar and Jupiter for their slaves. When James Kelley applied for a disability pension after the Civil War, he listed his children as dependents and had to verify his daughter's name. He named her Florilla, but her birth certificate lists her as Lovilla — the doctor wrote the incorrect name on the birth certificate.

New names are being created all the time. Wendy is a fairly popular girl's name in the United States, but it did not exist before the author J. M. Barrie invented it for a character in Peter Pan in 1904. Other names evolve from older names. Alice, the modern version of the medieval name Adelaide, became prevalent after the publication of *Alice in Wonderland* in 1865.

In the United States, middle names or surnames are commonly used as first names. A middle name may help distinguish between similarly named individuals. Many German Protestant and Catholic families used to name all the girls Maria or Mary. Their middle names differed so that people could tell them apart. A middle name is sometimes the mother's maiden name. In some cultures, there are several middle names before the surname, which can cause confusion. For example, in 1872, an immigration officer trying to list all the passengers who had arrived on a ship from Portugal neglected to write out full names. Therefore the entire list today provides only a first and a middle name, and no surnames!

Nicknames have also been used to distinguish people of the same name in the same family or town. Nicknames are often shorter versions of first names — for example Jim, Jimmy, or Jamie for James and Hank for Henry. Nicknames can also remind people of certain characteristics of the person, such as Slim. Some nicknames don't seem to have a particular meaning, like the names Butch and Spike. There are also nicknames for surnames. A popular shortened version of Sullivan is Sully, for instance.

The names of things and people change over time and reflect the era in which people lived. The words and names used in each generation may be clues to an ancestor's origins. By following such clues we may learn about the things that were important to our ancestors.

Focus on place names

Just as people have names and nicknames, so do geographic features and places. Our ancestors used place names to identify where they lived. These names sometimes changed over time, making it difficult to locate them.

Some locations in the United States originally had Native American names. The original name of Millis, Massachusetts, was Boggastowe before legislation changed it to the last name of a prominent citizen. Other places still retain their Native American names, like the village of Quononochataug.

The places where ancestors lived may be unrecognizable to a researcher. They may no longer be in existence, for many small towns disappeared into larger ones. Colonial maps may assist in locating these places. Current maps and gazetteers help people locate places if they still exist today. A gazetteer is a dictionary of place names. It lists the location of a place and occasionally the map coordinates, and it might give the meaning of the word and all of its usages. Sophisticated Web sites can also help an individual find a current locality.

Gazetteers and maps may not be able to help researchers find a site if they have only a nickname. "The Farms" referred to the town of Millis in colonial days and appeared in correspondence, but it does not appear in a gazetteer and can be found only on colonial maps. A dictionary of place nicknames can help. Each state has an official nickname, but many have unofficial names as well. Alaska was called America's Ice Box and the Frozen Wilderness because Americans once thought it was covered in ice year round. The city of Chicago has at least ten nicknames, including Tower City, Pork City, and the Windy City.

A public library is a good place to start your research.

5. Where to Find Help

"I remember being overwhelmed by my first visit to the public library. I didn't know where to look or even how to start my research. My public library had a local history collection, but my family was from a different part of the country. Luckily, the reference librarian pointed me in the right direction and taught me how to use the card catalog. In the reference section of the library, I found a list of all the libraries in the United States. The librarians also ordered books and articles I needed for my research from other libraries and helped me locate the addresses of other places that might be able to assist me. Once I apologized for asking so many questions, but the reference librarian told me that answering questions was his job."

Kathy started her research at a public library that was close to her house. The librarians helped Kathy discover the vast resources available to people who are researching genealogy. They taught her how to use reference books, periodicals, and other types of libraries and archives. Kathy learned that most libraries have periodicals or magazines, reference books, newspapers, scrapbooks, vertical files, and a local history collection. The first step in getting to know a library is to ask a reference librarian for an overview of the library's materials for genealogists.

Public libraries usually have magazine or periodical collections for popular publications, but you may have to order genealogical magazine articles through the librarians. Most genealogical and historical societies publish magazines. The PERiodical Source Index, or PERSI, is a guide to genealogical articles published from 1847 to the present. The material is organized by surname and place. PERSI is available in book form, microfiche, or CD-ROM. A library may not have this in their collection but it can be found in larger public libraries, genealogical societies, and Family History Centers. One can also access it for a small monthly fee through a Web site.

A reference book can provide a quick answer to a question. A good genealogical reference book will outline the records that exist and where to obtain them. Be sure to ask about the availability of electronic reference sources. Books in the reference section offer definitions of words and names. You can find a background history of the states, countries, or ethnic groups in the reference section of a public library.

Back copies of newspapers published in the area may be available on microfilm at the library. Newspapers contain notices of births, deaths, and marriages. News-papers are an excellent source because they provide details on what was happening on the day an ancestor was born; then you can place that person in historical perspective.

Some librarians maintain scrapbooks or indexes of local events or people. This information, gleaned from newspapers and magazines, is arranged chronologically or by subject.

Vertical files hold information about local individuals and happenings. Vertical files are found in a filing cabinet. The material is arranged as it would be in an index. This particular type of file provides information on local events and commonly asked questions.

Vertical files, scrapbooks, and indexes are often in a local history collection. The library may maintain a file or house the collection for the local historical society. This material may be found in the reference department; in larger libraries, it may be set aside in its own room.

While public libraries are an important place to begin research, it won't be long before you'll want to use a special library

Special libraries, like the New England Historic Genealogical Society in Boston, focus on genealogy.

or an archive. These are institutions that focus on a particular type of collection. It may be that an archive has material on the state or county in which you are interested. Some special libraries have collections of a particular type, such as maps or newspapers. Before using a special library or archive, write or phone them to determine if they have the necessary material. Then prepare a list of questions before your visit so that you can make the most of your research trip. Make sure to bring pencils and notecards on a visit. Please keep in mind that there are rules for using special libraries. The librarians will explain their rules for using the facility, including whether or not material can be photocopied.

A type of special library is a historical or genealogical society. They probably maintain a library of material on families that settled in the area. They usually also subscribe to periodicals of interest to genealogists and historians. One can also take classes for beginning genealogists.

Major genealogical libraries in the United States

National Genealogical Society
4527 17th St. North
Arlington, VA 22207
(703) 525-0050
www.ngsgenealogy.org
• *Membership includes the right to borrow books from their library. Their card catalog is available online.*

New England Historic and
Genealogical Society
101 Newbury St.
Boston, MA 02116
(617) 536-5740
www.nehgs.org
• *Members can borrow books from their
circulating library. You can access the
card catalog through their home page.*

The Family History Library
35 North West Temple
Salt Lake City, UT 84150
(800) 346-6044
• *Call for a list of their local centers.*

National Archives (NARA)
Pennsylvania Ave. at 8th St. NW
Washington, DC 20408
(800) 788-6282
www.nara.gov
• *NARA offers a free publication called
Aids for Genealogical Research. You can
borrow microfilms of NARA material by
ordering directly from them.*

Library of Congress
1st-2nd Sts. NW
Washington, DC 20006
www.loc.gov
• *You can check their online catalog for
materials that might apply.*

Allen County Public Library
900 Webster St.
P.O. Box 2270
Fort Wayne, IN 46801
(219) 424-7241
www.acpl.lib.in.us/genealogy/
genealogy.html
• *Their Web site is an online guide to
their collections and provides access to
their card catalog.*

Lineage and church or synagogue libraries are other types of special libraries. A lineage organization such as the Daughters of the American Revolution or the Society of Colonial Wars may have a library that the public can use for a fee. If one of your ancestors was a member of a lineage organization, contact a local chapter to ask what resources are available.

Archives and other research centers usually have rules regarding the use of their materials. Be sure to prepare for your visit in advance.

The largest church library is that of the Mormons, formally known as the Church of Jesus Christ of Latter-day Saints (LDS), located in Salt Lake City. The Mormons aided and advanced genealogical research by making great amounts of information readily available. They opened libraries in every state and published some of their resources on CD-ROM and microfiche. By using an affiliated library (an LDS Family History Center), you can, for a small fee, borrow films of records from all over the world. The resources of the Family History Centers are easy to use, and you can usually ask volunteers to assist you.

LDS resources on CD-ROM and microfiche

Ancestral File. This is a database created from information contributed by both church and nonchurch members. It can create pedigree charts.

International Genealogical Index. This lists birth, christening, and marriage information. Death records are not included.

Military Index. This is a list of individuals who died in the Korean and Vietnam Wars from 1950 to 1975. Birth and death dates and last place of residence for deceased persons appear here. You can also find out the place of death and rank and service number. There is additional information for Vietnam casualties.

Family History Library Catalog. This is the card catalog of the Family History Library. It describes the materials that are available at the library in Salt Lake City. Most of this material can be borrowed through a local Family History Center.

Social Security Death Index. If a relative had a social security number and his or her death was reported to the Social Security Administration after 1962, the death might be listed here. The CD includes date of birth (if known), state where social security card was issued, and place of residence at time of death.

While a trip to the library may not provide specific dates and family information, it will help researchers outline the context of their ancestors' lives. The individuals a family historian meets while conducting research are the best resources for information and assistance. Many genealogists consider librarians their friends because they provide invaluable research guidance.

Focus on city directories

A city directory is a listing of most of the adult residents in that location. It can include their address and occupation. Unlike the U.S. census, which occurs once every ten years, city directories are generally updated every one to two years. This can be very helpful, especially if an ancestor disappeared between censuses. If a family lived in a town or urban area, you should look at directories. Often several smaller communities will be included in one directory.

There are several parts to a directory. In the front, there is usually a listing of all the current street names and any changes in street names since the last volume. A map of the city or town will be either in the front or back of the volume. The central part of the book will be a listing of the residents of the city or town. Generally, this is just the adult working members of the household. Earlier directories included only men and widows, while marginalized communities, such as African Americans, were often listed separately. The back of the volume lists advertisements and business notices. It may contain an advertisement for an ancestor's business.

Another valuable section of the city directories are the lists of clubs and newspapers. If an ancestor played a musical instrument, you might be able to locate the name of a club to which he belonged. The local historical society can then help you locate other material, such as programs that relate to the group.

The types of information listed in a directory vary. Although there are inaccuracies and omissions, directories are a good source of material on the area they cover. They can include listings of churches, fire departments, post offices, and even teachers. Some individuals receive notice in a directory for other reasons — William Burbeck of Salisbury, Massachusetts, attracted attention because he lived to be eighty-two years old.

These volumes track people's movements from house to house, between communities, or through different occupa-

City directories can help you track a person over time. Such directories often have several sections that provide business listings.

tions. This can be a fascinating way to learn about your ancestors' lives.

The Library of Congress has the largest collection of city directories, and many smaller historical societies and town halls also keep collections of the directories for their area. Some institutions loan microfiche of city directories to individuals for a small fee.

Internet access is readily available through many public libraries.

6. Helpful Technology

When people think about genealogical research, they imagine dusty archives filled with documents. The reality is that although places like this exist, research today involves computers and other technologies.

"The first time someone showed me the World Wide Web, I couldn't believe that so much work could be done from home. I thought that once I finished all my local research, it would be much harder to find information. My uncle taught me how to search the Web for material on our family. It was incredible to think people could share research this way." Susan quickly learned how to communicate with other researchers by computer. "I sent an E-mail to people with the same last name requesting data on one of my ancestors and received replies from other people researching the same name. My uncle cautioned me not to accept everything people sent me until I had verified the data myself." Susan's uncle also reminded her not to forget the basics of genealogical research when using her computer.

The World Wide Web created a new way of conducting research — through search engines such as Yahoo or AltaVista or a service such as America Online (AOL). A search engine seeks out words or phrases that match a request. A search for the word *"genealogy"* yields thousands of sites. It is difficult to know which Web pages are the best. It's best to begin with a specific search and then go to a more general topic if you're unsuccessful.

Susan discovered that there are different types of Web sites. They fall into several categories: indexes, informational, and commercial. Web pages usually include links to other similar sites, so that the Web may be used as a reference library.

Some individuals create Web sites to index the best pages. These indexes are usually organized by category, which helps researchers filter out those sites that are not very helpful.

A person researching his family from outside his local area can find help through the United States GenWeb. This project supports free informational sites for all fifty states. In 1996, a group of volunteers began putting genealogical reference material for the United States on the Internet. The first site was for Kentucky. If you are looking for cemetery records, check the resource page to find out where the information is located or the name of a local person to contact. More material is being added all the time. Many foreign archives and libraries are putting material on their home page for people to use. In some cases, actual data is available.

Individuals can create their own home pages to make genealogical material and pictures of their family available to the public. It is becoming easier to create a personal Web site from construction kits found on the Web.

There are some sites that are both informational and commercial. These can be either reference tools or home pages created by individuals. The reference resources can resemble a good reference book or library. Susan discovered virtual libraries on the Web that provide information. Some of these charged a small fee, but others were free. Most of the fee-based services require a credit card. A Web site created by Ancestry Incorporated offers access to a wide variety of data.

Book publishers that specialize in genealogical and historical materials have created online book catalogs for their products. Using these sites, Susan created a bibliography of books that she wanted to examine. She was then able to search library card catalogs on the Internet to see which libraries owned them. Public librarians she knew could borrow the books she needed from other libraries. She built a research plan using card catalogs on the Internet.

Susan discovered that several national libraries have their card catalogs online, on the Internet. Among them are the New England Historic Genealogical Society, the National Genealogical Society, the Allen County Public Library, and the Library of Congress. It is even possible to borrow books over the Internet. Both the New England Historic Genealogical Society and the National Genealogical Society lend books to members for a fee. Susan wanted to meet other people researching her family, so she submitted

National Genealogical Society

Family Chronicle
The Magazine for Families Researching Their Roots

Welcome

1999 NGS CONFERENCE IN THE STATES
RICHMOND, VIRGINIA 12–15 MAY 1999 VIRGINIA

Welcome to the 95 year old National Genealogical Society. Unlike many mature organizations we're getting younger every year.

We were founded in 1903. It was a marvelous year with an atmosphere of excitement and adventure that filled every day. For example, it's the year that Henry Ford founded the Ford Motor Company; Dr. Charles Harrod Campbell became the first president of NGS; J.P. Morgan founded the International Mercantile Marine Company; and the first coast to coast crossing of an American car took place (65 days). One more cuddly thing, the first teddy bear was designed and named after Teddy Roosevelt. It was a great time for dreams.

As we prepare for our 100th birthday, NGS continues to be exciting and we are still dreamers. This new website is a good example of our willingness —not only to dream, but also to take action.

While NGS has always provided great service to our members, we are dedicated to doing an even better job for you. Take a little arm chair tour of our new interactive website. Let me know what you think, and remember —great new ideas are always appreciated.

If you are among the many thousands who are NGS members, we thank you for your support. Those of you who are at the threshold of joining our family, we welcome you.

You, too, can grow younger with us, as we all explore the past with the miracle tools of today.

Fran Shane
Executive Director

The National Genealogical Society has a variety of materials accessible at their Web site.

her request through a news group and included her home address and her Internet address. News groups for genealogy can be found at the address www. soc.genealogy. Your request should provide specific names and dates. Susan received queries from other people as well as answers to her questions.

She also sent E-mail to libraries and archives describing her research problems, and she received advice and some family history via E-mail. An advantage to services like AOL is that the company sponsors interest groups that allow people to discuss their hobby in an online chat room.

As you do your research, you will become familiar with microfilm, microfiche, and CD-ROMs. In order to preserve documents in their collections, many archives are microfilming heavily used materials so that the original can be protected. CD-ROMs resemble music CDs in appearance but contain data instead of music.

Today it is easier to conduct genealogical research, due to CD-ROMs and the Internet. However, researchers should use the information found in these two sources cautiously. Mistakes appear in all types of research material (including original documents). A good genealogist always tries to double check data in a variety of sources. You should create a research log as you use the new technologies. Web addresses change frequently, and CDs are updated. It is good to know not only when a site or CD was consulted but also its address and the date. Susan made use of all the resources — electronic, print, and original — to research her family. By doing so, she was able to enrich her family story with the variety of materials she was able to find.

A glossary of technology

E-mail: A message sent electronically from one computer to another.

Home page: A Web page that introduces a viewer to organizations, companies, or individuals.

Listserv or news group: An electronic discussion group. Listservs are available over the Usenet through an Internet provider.

Microfilm or microfiche: A type of film used in a special viewer that allows a person to look at copies of documents.

Search engine: An electronic index of Web sites that allows a user to locate sites on a particular topic or subject.

Usenet: Allows you to send and receive messages over the Internet. Usenet differs technologically from E-mail.

Web sites

www.cyndislist.com
Cyndi's List of Genealogy Sites on the Internet.
• This site links over 21,000 Web pages organized by category and cross-referenced.

www.ancestry.com
Ancestry's Home Town.
• This site provides more than a hundred searchable databases, some of which are free.

www.genealogy.tbox.com
Helm's Genealogy Toolbox.
• This acts as an index to other Web sites for genealogists.

www.cpcug.org/user/jlacombe/mark.html
Barrel of Genealogy Links.
• This is an online index similar to Cyndi's List and Helm's Toolbox.

www. genweb.org
United States GenWeb.
• Free information on genealogical resources within the United States.

Immigrants came to America for a variety of reasons. Ask members of your family if there are any stories relating to immigrant experiences.

7. A Land of Many Cultures

"My great-grandfather immigrated to Hawaii from Japan to work in the pineapple fields," began Scott. "In three short generations, my family background became ethnically diverse and multicultural. My grandfather left Hawaii to study at a university in the Midwest. While in school he met my grandmother, who was of German ancestry. My father was born there." Scott's father met and married a woman descended from an old American family. "The history of my family is part of the history of the United States," Scott continued. Four generations of his family traveled across the country and intermarried with individuals from a variety of backgrounds.

People settled in America for various reasons. Some sought religious and political freedom; others hoped for economic opportunities. Some ethnic groups did not come here voluntarily but were sent here as slaves or indentured servants. Many immigrants experienced incredible adventures and also faced hardships. Imagine leaving family and everything familiar behind to live in a completely foreign place, where you might not even speak the language! The period in which immigrants arrived in America depended on their reasons for immigrating and their original homeland. In the colonial period ships brought slaves from Africa and the West Indies. Millions of Irish emigrated in the 1840s to escape starvation during the

Great Potato Famine of the 1840s; this famine resulted in widespread disease and death in Ireland. Italians, Greeks, and Russians started arriving in the United States in the late nineteenth century. Today, people are immigrating from Eastern Europe, Southeast Asia, and Central and South America. Family members might remember when the first members of their family arrived and where they settled. In the nineteenth century, a woman wrote to her sister in Germany asking her to send one of her sons to America. The woman's only son had died in the Civil War, and she needed help on the farm. None of her nephews wanted to go, but their sister did. She traveled from Germany to Wisconsin by herself at the age of fourteen.

Immigrants discovered that everyday routines differed in their new settlements. The more rural the settlement, the harder a family had to work to survive. Men and women worked alongside one another in the field to plant crops because of a labor shortage. The things that we take for granted such as heat, food, clothes, and cleanliness were not readily available. Women on the frontier raised sheep to make cloth and created dyes from plants. Bathing could be a luxury when water was scarce. Nature was a danger on the frontier. A woman settler in Alaska in the early twentieth century wrote that it was cold enough in her cabin to freeze food before it could be cooked. Blizzards could last days and leave a family unable to provide for itself.

Urban newcomers faced different challenges. Families often lived together in a single apartment, and work could be scarce. Whether the immigrants settled in the city or on the frontier, social visits from friends and relatives provided relief from everyday struggles. Even in the smallest villages, people gathered to hold dances and celebrate holidays, such as the Fourth of July.

It may be difficult to research a particular heritage due to language, circumstances, or religion. It may be necessary to research the immigration of a particular

Immigration also refers to resettlement within the United States. Individuals traveled to seek opportunity in other parts of the country.

ethnic group to this country, the history of the area where a family settled, and the culture of the group. Listen to a family's oral traditions to discover clues about its heritage, and then set out to prove their accuracy. In some cultures, oral traditions exist rather than written records. A good language dictionary can help you decipher the foreign words you encounter on standard documents such as birth, marriage, and death certificates. Become familiar with the culture and history of the ethnic group being researched. Think of a family in its historical context. Be careful

not to make quick judgments. Not all African Americans before the Civil War were slaves or lived on plantations. Be sure to verify the data found in records.

Immigration refers to individuals traveling across a country as well as from other countries. There are many different types of records to help you locate your ancestors, such as vital records, census records, passenger lists, letters, diaries and journals, reminiscences, photographs, newspapers, church records, business records, and fraternal societies. The sources for immigration research provide more personal information about ancestors and their daily lives.

Birth, marriage, and death records may not exist due to the history of the area or the ethnic group. It might not be possible to locate a marriage certificate for some members of a family because the marriage might not have been officially recorded. You may discover that prior to a certain generation genealogical information is hard to locate due to slavery or relocation. When you do find records they may be in another language.

After consulting home sources like letters, diaries, and photographs, census records are a good place to start. Since 1790, the U.S. government has taken a census of the country's inhabitants every ten years. All censuses after 1850 list the name of every member of the household and his or her place of birth. Several generations of relatives often lived in a single household. Cousins, aunts, uncles, grandparents, and children often lived in extended households. A family's children might be born in different states as they traveled across the country. You might also learn the names of relatives you did not know existed. Census takers often listed Native Americans as black. They also attributed the ethnicity of the head of the household to the entire family, even if the family was interracial or of different ethnicities. Try to find an additional source before accepting any information. The 1900 census asked individuals for their year of immigration. You can use this date to locate a passenger list.

Passenger lists can show all passengers on a particular ship or all individuals crossing the borders of Canada or Mexico on a given day. Joseph Bessette crossed the Canadian border at Vermont in 1918. In order to enter the United States he had to state his occupation, age, place of birth, and name of his nearest relative and the town in which he or she lived. The customs officer also recorded the color of his eyes, hair, and complexion, as well as his height, for identification purposes. It may be that the first record that you locate is information about an ancestor's travels as well as the immigration documents. Joseph Bessette regularly traveled to Canada to visit the family he left behind. His border crossings recorded the name and address of his brother living in Canada. The date of an ancestor's arrival in America can influence the type of information you can discover. A passenger list from the 1820s may only provide the name, citizenship, and final destination of an ancestor, but even this can be helpful. It may be that a single member of a family immigrated to the United States to start a family farm or that fourteen members arrived in the same city for eventual settlement elsewhere in the country.

Newspapers often carried advertisements encouraging families to settle in a particular state. These notices inspired individuals with claims of opportunities for both the farmer and the businessperson. A Minnesota newspaper printed an editorial hoping to entice farmers to settle there, but it claimed that physicians would not find many patients because of the healthy climate. That same editorial encouraged young women (but only those who worked hard) to move to Minnesota.

The economic security of the family was dependent on all members of a household working together. John Muir, a Scottish immigrant and later an explorer and naturalist, recalled his boyhood on his father's farm as consisting of long days filled with strenuous labor.

Letters and diaries also offer insights into the daily lives of settlers and immigrants. Several members of a community would often immigrate to the new country, settle in the same area, and intermarry.

Immigrants often settled in areas where individuals of the same ethnic background were living.

Maria Little Kendall migrated to Illinois with her husband and corresponded frequently with her sister in Vermont. "Being so far away from home, parents and land of my nativity is all I have to regret. I have become considerable [sic] acquainted with my neighbors. Specially those from the same state as myself. There are five Vermont families that live within a half mile of us, all in sight."

One of the first things many immigrants would do when they arrived in the United States was to join or establish a church or synagogue. Going to church or temple was a central part of life in the new country. It provided the settlers an opportunity to meet as a community and socialize. Settlers could meet to worship in their native language. Church also provided settlers with a place to share news of the old country. Ask your relatives if there was a family place of worship. Baptism and marriage records can help a researcher establish a relationship between members of a community. Some close-knit communities maintained church and Bible records in their native language after they arrived in the United States.

The religious affiliation of individuals can lead to new sources of information.

Records created by churches and synagogues can help you learn about the relationships between individuals.

Many churches kept good records. If a family's ancestry is Hispanic, church records will be extremely important. Missions often maintained records of baptisms, marriages, first communions, and students who attended the mission school. Catholic churches often included the woman's maiden name on the marriage document. Each maiden name leads a researcher to another line of the family.

Many immigrants became U.S. citizens by applying to be naturalized. Naturalization certificates list basic facts about the applicant such as name, place of birth, date of immigration, and possibly the name of the ship. On the citizenship papers a man submitted in 1894 in Minnesota, he made an oath that he was born in Norway in 1872 and arrived in New York in July of 1891. Application papers include a statement from someone who knew an ancestor and vouched for his character. These papers may document family names, relatives, and previous residences.

Government records can be helpful.

After the Civil War, the U.S. government operated a Freedmen's Bureau to help African Americans adjust to life after slavery. The bureau recorded marriages, apprenticeships, labor contracts, and lists of individuals in need of financial assistance. This material is maintained by the National Archives in Washington, D.C. In areas of the country that were not originally part of the United States, notarial records are an important resource. Notaries recorded marriages, sales of goods, apprenticeships, dowries, and wills.

There are special research collections located in libraries or genealogical societies for specific ethnic groups. By contacting a facility that collects material on an ethnic group, one can make contacts with other individuals interested in the same family or discover new materials to examine.

While the search for a cultural and ethnic heritage is challenging, you will learn more about your family and be able to incorporate new traditions into your life. A family history becomes more interesting

While searching for information on relatives, you may discover that they belonged to a fraternal organization.

with each new discovery. The search for an immigrant or ethnic ancestor is often the most important one for many genealogists because it connects them to another country and a new realm of research.

Special collections

Schomberg Center for Research in Black Culture
515 Malcolm X Blvd.
New York, NY 10051

• *This library is a branch of the New York Public Library. It maintains a collection of genealogies of African American families.*

American Jewish Archives
3101 Clifton Ave.
Cincinnati, OH 45220
• *Some of the collections in this institution are available on interlibrary loan.*

For additional ethnic archives and special libraries, consult the American Library Association's *American Library Directory.* This is available at most public libraries.

Focus on newspapers

The first newspapers printed in the United States were similar to today's newspapers in many ways. There was a news section, advertisements, and marriage and death announcements in every issue. However, early newspapers were shorter than today's papers, consisting of only a few pages. Small towns often published only one weekly newspaper, while a city like New York published hundreds of daily and weekly papers. Ethnic groups in the United States often published newspapers in their own language. For instance, the first French newspaper in the United States appeared in Newport, Rhode Island, in 1780. Ethnically diverse areas like New York City supported multiple papers for large ethnic groups.

Newspapers provided immigrants with news from their homeland and information on activities within their ethnic community. This can help researchers learn more about what life was like for their ancestors. Certain newspapers, like the *Boston Pilot,* circulated nationally and ran a column devoted to locating family members who had disappeared in the United States. Personal notices appeared in most newspapers to keep the community informed about who married or died, but also included advertisements about runaway slaves, servants, and family members. Foreign language communities still publish newspapers today.

The United States Newspaper Project is trying to create a database of all the newspapers published in the United States. Each state has a coordinator for the project. The master list of newspapers is available through most public libraries. An easy way to locate a list of the newspapers published in a particular area is to consult a city directory for that town and then ask a librarian where copies are available. If the newspaper is available on microfilm, a library might be able to borrow the appropriate reels through interlibrary loan. Two of the largest collections of newspapers are at the Library of Congress in Washington, D.C., and the American Antiquarian Society in Worcester, Massachusetts.

Family members often talk about military service or patriotic deeds.

8. Wartime America

David began researching his own genealogy when he was seven. "My grandmother used to tell me stories about members of her family, especially her uncle who served in the Civil War. One day I started asking her questions about the people she mentioned and a photograph fell out of a book she was holding. 'Who is that a picture of?' I asked her. She told me it was her father, my great-grandfather. The book she was holding was a genealogy of her family that was written before she was born. I got very excited and ran to get a piece of paper and a pencil so that I could take notes. I still have those original notes."

David continued to sit with his grandmother and to ask questions about her family. "The next chance I got, I went to the public library and asked the reference librarian if I could look at the local history collection." By looking in the published vital records of his town, David discovered the dates of birth, death, and marriage for several members of his grandmother's family. "I suddenly realized that the people she told me about were real and had lived actual lives. The more I learned, the more I wanted to know." David's research revealed that members of his grandmother's family fought in almost every American war, from King Phillip's War in 1676 to World War II.

As David learned, almost every generation of Americans has been involved in wartime activities in one way or another.

By comparing the dates of your ancestors with a list of military events, you may discover ancestors who actually participated in several military conflicts in their lifetime.

Checklist of military events

Colonial conflicts: 1676–1763
Revolutionary War: 1776–1783
War of 1812: 1812–1815
Mexican-American War: 1846–1848
Civil War: 1861–1865
Spanish-American War: 1898
World War I: 1917–1918
World War II: 1941–1945
Korean War: 1950–1953
Vietnam War: 1961–1972

Once you've identified the wars in which your ancestors may have served, you can access sources such as military service records and pension applications. It is important to know that not all clues appear in the military records. An ancestor may have escaped notice in the official records, but diaries, letters, photographs, reminiscences, newspaper notices, and biographies can fill in the blanks. Be sure to ask family members for their advice and for any stories of military service. You may find out that an ancestor wore a colorful Zouave uniform, complete with a red cap, during the Civil War, or, as David did, that a grandmother served doughnuts to soldiers while serving for the Red Cross. If you don't find information immediately, keep looking.

Although military service typically involved male family members, one can miss an interesting story about a female relative by limiting research to the men in a family. For instance, during the Revolutionary War, Deborah Sampson felt it was her patriotic duty to enlist, and she did so under the alias of Robert Shurtleff. She was one of only a few women to receive a military pension for Revolutionary War service. Some women served as spies and nurses, and others accompanied their sons and husbands into battle in order to be near them. One soldier's mother followed

Look beyond the males' roles in your family so that you don't miss out on the contributions of the women and children.

his regiment in order to help with his laundry.

Children also contributed to the war effort. In the American Revolution and the Civil War, twelve-year-old boys served as regimental drummers and young girls helped their mothers with fundraising enterprises. Schoolchildren formed clubs that supported war efforts through their activities. During the Civil War, a group of children created a quilt and dedicated it,

"For any soldier who loves little children."

The first places to look for evidence of an ancestor's wartime activities are military service records and pension records. Service records from the Revolutionary War and Civil War generally include facts such as name, rank, unit one served in, date of enlistment, and possibly place of birth. Pension applications, on the other hand, are stories in the soldiers' own words: they often contain detailed information about soldiers' lives and their military service. In his Revolutionary War pension application, Armintus Weeden recalled that his master, Peleg Carr, placed him in the U.S. army. According to the pension documents, this former slave was thirteen years old at the time of his military service.

Pension records can fill in the blanks in a family story. In his great-uncle's pension records, David discovered details that even family members did not know. He learned that his great-uncle had joined the Civil War at the age of sixteen and was blinded in a gun-cleaning accident.

Many soldiers returned home with battle wounds, and just as many returned with chronic illnesses such as diarrhea and malaria due to the harsh living conditions during war and the lack of sanitary facilities. More than one soldier claimed that sleeping on the wet ground during the Civil War crippled him. Others attributed disabilities to excessive exposure to the sun. One soldier applied for a medical pension because a bug crawled into his

ear. These testimonies may seem amusing today, but in an era when the causes of illness were not clearly understood, these soldiers' accounts were taken seriously.

Diaries and letters are also a good resource when you are trying to learn more about an ancestor. A soldier wrote

Diaries and letters can help you understand the experience of ancestors and relatives who served.

that he entered the army out of love for his country. Not all soldiers would agree with those sentiments. Soldiers witnessed the horrors of war and described atrocities in their letters. Soldiers in the field had to sleep on the ground regardless of the weather. Housing, when available, was far from luxurious. Heat was scarce. Often one heater would provide warmth for eighty or ninety men. They always ate outside, even in the winter. Regiments usually consisted of men from a particular town, so letters home contained news about the death of a friend or neighbor. Correspondence from other soldiers in an ancestor's regiment may provide details about that ancestor.

Letters that Civil War soldiers sent and received often included a *carte de visite,* a small photograph. The small photos were popular at the time of the Civil War. These photos could fit in an envelope and were inexpensive to purchase. Photographers often traveled to the battlefields to take pictures of the soldiers in the field. If you have a Civil War photograph, you may be able to identify the regiment in which an ancestor served from the uniform in the picture.

After serving in a war, many veterans felt the need to record their war experiences for future generations. Most wartime narratives are dramatic battle descriptions. J. Alberts Monroe recounted that at the First Battle of Bull Run he felt a shot pass by his body and then saw it knock his commanding officer off his horse. He was very surprised to see his captain jump back on his horse, stating, "That about took my breath away." The bullet had narrowly missed him.

Soldiers also included details about what they ate. One soldier told a humorous account of a cooking incident on an old battlefield. Their cook unknowingly buried their bean pot over an unexploded shell, and the heat from the fire caused the beans and the shell to explode. One of his fellow soldiers remarked that beans are quite lively when cooked!

Many reminiscences are not as humorous and include details of the soldier's life before military service. Samuel Downing began his story with his kidnapping as a child before the Revolutionary War. He told about the day his parents left him at home to play with his friends. A man approached and asked if anyone would like to learn the trade of making spinning wheels. Samuel said that he did want to learn, not realizing that he would never see his family again. After he went with the man, Samuel was so homesick that he went into the woods and cried. When the war broke out, he ran away from the man who had kidnapped him and joined the militia.

Other soldiers wrote about their service with famous generals such as George Washington. Alexander Milliner remembered that as the regiment was marching, General Washington saw some boys playing a game with stones and ordered a halt to the march. Washington decided to participate in the game. He beat them all and smiled, but he did not laugh at the boys.

Newspapers often ran notices and advertisements about specific individuals.

Colonial newspapers regularly published notices of Revolutionary War deserters, for instance. These notices typically include a deserter's birth place or age, last residence, regiment in the army, and occupation. They often contained detailed physical descriptions. For example, John Rynes, a Revolutionary War deserter, was born in Ireland, stood about five feet eleven and a half inches tall, had light eyes, sandy hair, and freckles. John Brown was five and a half feet high, with a thin nose and a long, narrow face.

A researcher may find news articles about an ancestor's patriotism, an extensive obituary, or simply an interesting story. In one case, a Civil War soldier clutched a photograph of three young children as he died on a battlefield. The person who found him could not identify the man and notify his family, so he wrote to newspaper publishers and asked them to publish the picture of the children. It was through reading one of these stories that the soldier's wife learned he was dead.

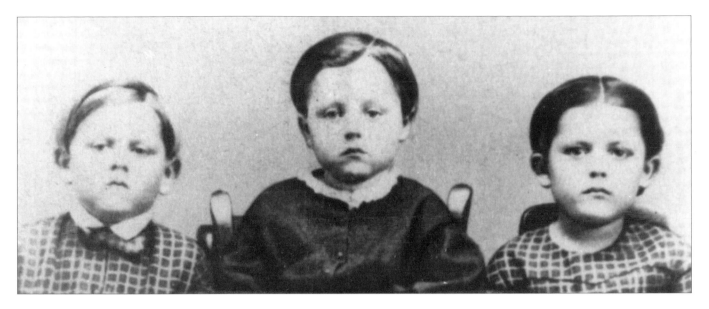

Amos Humiston died on a Civil War battlefield clutching a photograph of his three children.

Many schools and universities published tributes to their students who served in major wars. These volumes often exaggerate the facts, but they can be a wonderful way to learn more about the person behind the facts. The biographies contain information about an ancestor's military service and also about his family and his school and civic activities. Sullivan Ballou's life is recounted in Brown University's history of students in the Civil War. His biography includes very detailed information on his childhood and his family. In order to supplement the financial support his uncle gave him to attend Brown, Sullivan taught school and also taught flute lessons during school vacations. Only a small part of his biography was devoted to his military service and the fact that he died in battle.

David's inquiry into his family's military heritage was successful because he used the resources available to him. Remember that the types of documents available depend on the time period of the military event.

Sullivan Ballou's university paid him tribute for his military service.

Focus on cemeteries

On Memorial Day there are cemetery ceremonies to honor the men and women who fought in America's military conflicts. During these ceremonies, a metal marker or flag is usually placed in front of each gravestone. These markers indicate that the person buried there was in the military. They identify the war the person served in and sometimes the branch of the military. Differently designed markers represent each war, and they can direct a researcher to additional information on that ancestor.

Several organizations commemorate military service with cemetery markers. The Grand Army of the Republic had placed medallions on the graves of Civil War soldiers. One can then locate material from the particular post and regiment to which an ancestor belonged. The American Legion places markers at the graves of soldiers from World War I to the present. If a female ancestor was a member of the Daughters of the American Revolution, she may have a symbol of the organization in front of her gravesite identifying her as a member. In order to qualify for membership in the Daughters of the American Revolution, one has to prove ancestry from a Revolutionary War soldier.

A clearinghouse of information on military cemeteries or those containing the graves of soldiers is maintained in each state. A list of cemeteries designated as historic may be found at the state historical society or archives.

Places to contact

The National Archives
Pennsylvania Ave. at 8th St. NW
Washington, DC 20408
(800) 788-6282
www.nara.gov
• *The National Archives offers a series of free brochures for the beginning genealogist and order forms for pension applications and military service records for the years 1776 through 1918.*

National Personnel Record Center
(Military Records) (NARA)
9700 Page Blvd.
St. Louis, MO 63132
• *This agency provides help with veterans' records dating from World War I.*

Daughters of the American Revolution
Library
1776 D St. NW

Washington, DC 20006-5392
(202) 879-3229
• *This library maintains files on membership applications submitted by women descended from Revolutionary War soldiers.*

It is important to organize your project around a specific idea. Ask relatives about the details of their lives.

9. A Personal Story

"I was trying to decide how to organize my family history project when my mom started to tell me about the dog she owned when she was my age. I asked her about other pets in the family and she had lots of stories. Some of my friends decided to use immigration as a theme in their project, while others used family recipes. I went back and interviewed some family members about their pets. One of my immigrant ancestors owned a dog called Little Watch, who kept him company on his travels across the frontier. Other family members related how animals on the farm doubled as companions. An aunt showed me a photograph of her riding in a wagon pulled by a goat. Her sister told me how one of the family dogs was re-lated to Fala, President Roosevelt's dog. She even wrote him a letter and enclosed a picture of her dog. My grandmother told me about her dog named Snowball whose fur was so white she would lose sight of it in the snow." Using pets to link the past with the present made Jenny's family history more meaningful to her than the names and dates she accumulated in her research.

You can continue to investigate and verify the facts of your family by tracing every relative in a family tree. At some point you'll want to put it all together in a book or project. Remember that this is a personal story. A presentation is an expression of your family. Jenny is fascinated by animals and stories about them.

She used this interest as the theme of her family history. If you have any special artistic talents, you may want to think about how to represent a family in art. In the nineteenth century it was quite common for girls to create memorials to their families by creating a tree in needlework or watercolor. Each member of the family is represented by a heart or an apple with the dates he or she was born and died. They could be quite beautiful because of the layout and colors. Some family historians even used hair from their relatives in their trees!

As you review your research, it is important to think about the intended audience. Genealogy can be a personal pursuit or it can be passed on to other family members. You can focus on one particular aspect of your family history, such as the immigration experience, or compile a collection of your family's special recipes. Each project can be illustrated with pictures and biographical information. It may be that your family members are very athletic and their history is part of the history of sports. Perhaps relatives recall their early involvement

You may want to include stories of trips that your family members have taken.

with baseball in the late nineteenth century. You could include your own experiences with rollerblading or snowboarding. It may be that ancestors kept scrapbooks, created quilts, or left another type of legacy. In the process of searching for family lore and data, you may start a new tradition. Some families use their research to organize a family reunion. Regardless of how you choose to tell your story, be sure to include, either as part of the project or as a separate manuscript, an introduction, a bibliography, and a listing of family members.

The introduction describes what your story is about and can include a list of acknowledgments of people who have helped with the project. Here you explain how you organized your material. You can also explain how you started this project and why. For instance, is this project a novel based on family stories or a traditional genealogy?

The list of family members is an index to the material. One kind of list is called an Ahentafel, which is German for "ancestor table." It is a list of your direct ancestors

Remember to include information on all the members of your family.

that provides birth, marriage, and death dates and places.

A project should include a list of illustrations and who owns them. This allows researchers to contact those people in the future. In the same way, the bibliography and list of source notes or citations help other individuals retrace your steps.

As long as you document your research, you can include your source notes in a variety of places. Footnotes or citations can be placed at the bottom of the page or listed at the end of the book near

Some nineteenth-century genealogists depicted their family as a tree. The immigrant ancestor was the trunk.

the bibliography. When you write a family story, you should include citation or source notes, because they are helpful for the next person researching the family.

The bibliography lists all the books, magazines, CD-ROMs, Web sites, and interviews consulted. The bibliography in this book is a guide on how to cite sources in project bibliographies.

Genealogies also include an explanation of the numbering system used in the project or book. In the Kelley family it is important to know which James Kelley

one is talking about, for there are seven generations of them! Look at other genealogies or books for ideas on how to number and how to organize the material. Many people create their own system. Remember that a genealogy should be easy for people other than its creator to use.

A traditional genealogy usually begins with the immigrant ancestor and moves forward in time. An alternative is to start with oneself and work backward. If you use a computer program to organize research, you may be able to choose from a variety of formats.

A project or book provides an opportunity to share research experiences and new information with others. A family history project describes the people and experiences that make a family unique.

Focus on handwriting

Researchers see many different styles of handwriting when trying to locate their ancestors and probably not all of it is legible. The ability to read other people's

Handwriting is taught as a part of formal education, although the way it is taught has changed over time. Compare your handwriting with that of other members of your family.

handwriting is a skill that develops with practice. If a document is difficult to decipher, study it to see if there are similar letters that are recognizable.

Time period, nationality, age, gender, and purpose influence the style of forming letters. A person's first language also affects the style of forming letters. Each of us has a distinctive style of handwriting. Compare your penmanship with that of your parents and ancestors. Handwriting styles differed between men and women and between formal and informal letters, diaries, and records. The study of handwriting is called paleography.

The education our ancestors received influenced their handwriting. Not everyone learned to write. Ideas of literacy also changed. Education varied in different parts of the country and in different time periods. The census after 1850 indicated whether a person attended school or could read and write.

Members of your family may have never learned to read or write, or they may have been literate only in their native language. Your ancestors may have identified themselves on documents by signing their mark. A mark may be a simple X or a more elaborate symbol that a person used to distinguish himself from others in place of a signature.

An ancestor's handwriting is as distinct as her life history. The way ancestors wrote is a reflection of when they lived and who they were.

Genealogy is **your** *own story, complete with surprises and ordinary events.*

10. Final Thoughts

Genealogy is one of the most popular hobbies in the United States. Newspapers and magazine articles focus on dramatic stories of people searching for family information and discovering famous relatives, secrets, and surprises. However, most people do not have this type of hidden past in their family. It is important to have patience when researching one's ancestors. If we always expect to find drama, we might overlook other, more interesting clues about a family history. We all should be proud of our heritage, no matter how ordinary it may seem to be.

Sarah was enthralled by the story of her family's trip to the United States. "My father told me a story that his grandfather repeated whenever he had the chance. It told how his parents arrived in Texas from Mexico. Each time, he told it exactly the same way. His parents wanted to escape the Mexican War and bought train tickets to travel to the border. At the Texas border, all the passengers on the train paid five cents to walk across a bridge into the United States. Everyone in the family tells the story the same way. The romance of my grandfather's family packing their belongings and starting a new life encouraged me to find out more." Sarah's great-grandfather created a family legend that has survived for generations.

Our genealogies connect us to our families through a shared heritage. It is a hobby for all generations. By contacting

Juliana Moore accompanied her husband to the Civil War and had her picture taken in uniform.

You may discover that your ancestors had hidden talents.

individuals to ask about our family history, we learn more about family relationships. Sarah has not been able to verify all the information in the story, but in the course of her research she met relatives whom she never knew.

The basic rule of genealogy is to start with the present and work backward in time from the known to the unknown. It is important to verify one piece of information before trying to locate the next. Many researchers have not followed the rules

and therefore mistakenly traced someone else's family tree.

Try not to think of genealogy in terms of gender and history. Researchers who think that only male members of their family did a certain type of work or saw military service overlook the contributions of women and children. Although it is easy to make assumptions about one's family, be sure to look beyond the obvious when conducting research.

Libraries can be a wonderful resource.

A historical context can uncover additional material. Use a dictionary to help you understand the meaning of words. Immigration is the story of people moving to the United States as well as traveling across the country. If you cannot locate something, it helps to go back and retrace steps. It is easy to miss a critical piece of information in one's excitement over a new discovery and to become distracted by an interesting document or bit of information. Charts and forms do help keep a person on track.

A good family detective always prepares for a research adventure by organizing notes and making a list of questions. While they might not discover any dramatic stories or events in their own family, individuals might meet people who have interesting stories to tell. Sarah knew her family legend and worked steadily to learn the names and dates of the individuals in her family. She learned about relatives still living in Mexico and wrote to them. Her family even planned a visit so that she could interview them.

It does not matter how a person becomes curious about his or her family. It is the sense of discovery and history that keeps us interested in the pursuit of stories and information. There are individuals who enjoy the genealogical quest so much that they decide to help others trace their families. The history of an individual is not only the story of a family, but is an integral part of the story of where we live and our history.

A sense of discovery keeps the family historian interested in the search.

Notes

The interviews presented at the beginning of each chapter are composites of conversations with the following people: Lynn Betlock, Kai Goto, George Hibbard, David Lambert, Marcia Melnyk, Jane Schwerdtfeger, Mary Lou Strong, Alice Taylor, and Susan Willey. Names have been changed.

Chapter 1: Our Families

Alex Haley's *Roots* (New York: Doubleday, 1976) created a new interest in family history. Other excellent books are Shirlee Taylor Haizlip's *The Sweeter the Juice: A Family Memoir in Black and White* (New York: Touchstone, 1994) and Joy Horowitz's *Tessie and Pearlie: A Granddaughter's Story* (New York: Macmillan, 1996).

Bertie L. Martin's diary is in the manuscript collection of the New England Historic Genealogical Society.

A *Newsweek* article titled "Family Secrets" focused on the personal detective aspect of family history. The article, written by Patricia King, Brad Stone, Peter Katel, and Theodore Gideonse, appeared in *Newsweek* on February 24, 1997, on pages 24 to 30.

Heraldry is difficult to explain, but Iain Moncrieffee and Don Pottinger's *Simple Heraldry: Cheerfully Illustrated* (Edinburgh: Thomas Nelson & Sons, 1953) is excellent. A more sophisticated approach is taken in Jullian Franklyn and John Tanner's *An Encyclopedic Dictionary of Heraldry* (New York: Pergamon Press, 1970).

Chapter 2: Family Stories and Keepsakes

Family artifacts can bring life to a family history. Russell D. Earnest's *Grandma's At-*

tic: *Making Heirlooms Part of Your Family History* (Albuquerque, N.M.: R. D. Earnest Associates, 1991) describes ways to make use of them. Barbara Sagraves's *A Preservation Guide: Saving the Past and Present for the Future* (Salt Lake City: Ancestry, 1995) demonstrates how to preserve family artifacts for future generations.

David Weitzman's *My Backyard History Book* (Boston: Little, Brown and Company, 1975) offers an assortment of activities to aid the research of a family or neighborhood. An important aspect of genealogy is the interviewing of relatives. *How to Tape Instant Oral Biographies* (New York: Guarionex Press, 1992) describes how one can create an oral history of a family.

Karen Frisch-Ripley's *Unlocking the Secrets in Old Photographs* (Salt Lake City: Ancestry, 1991) explains how to identify the people in family photos. A fascinating explanation of the clothing worn in photographs appears in *Dressed for the Photographer,* by Joan Severa (Kent, Ohio: Kent State University Press, 1996). *The Care and Identification of 19th Century Prints,* by

James M. Reilly (Rochester: Eastman Kodak, 1986), offers suggestions on how to preserve images and identify the processes used to create them.

Chapter 3: Getting Started

An extensive list of helpful sources is presented in Loretto Dennis Szucz and Sandra Hargreaves Luebking's *The Source: A Guidebook of American Genealogy* (Salt Lake City: Ancestry, 1996). A similar reference book is Alice Eicholz's *Ancestry's Red Book: American State, County, and Town Sources,* rev. ed. (Salt Lake City: Ancestry, 1992), which explains how to locate records. Thomas Kemp's *International Vital Record Handbook* (Baltimore: Genealogical Publishing, 1994) provides the necessary forms to order records. Free charts are available online at www.genrecords.com.

Examples of how to footnote research appear in Elizabeth Shown Mills, *Evidence! Citation and Analysis for the Family Historian* (Baltimore: Genealogical Publishing, 1997).

Chapter 4: What Does That Mean?

Both the *Random House Historical Dictionary of American Slang*, eds. J. E. Lighter, J. Ball, and J. O'Connor (New York: Random House, 1994) and *The Oxford Dictionary of New Words: A Popular Guide to Words in the News* (New York: Oxford University Press, 1991) are fascinating guides to the history of word usage. Barbara Jean Evans's *A to Zax: A Comprehensive Dictionary for Genealogists & Historians* (Alexandria, Va.: Hearthside Press, 1995) is excellent for discovering archaic phrases and occupations.

An online version of the names listed in the 1990 U.S. census is at www.census.gov/ftp/pub/genealogy/wab. An article on Li appeared in *Time* on May 19, 1997, on page 25.

A good source for understanding the derivation of surnames is Elsdon C. Smith's *New Dictionary of American Family Names* (New York: Harper & Row, 1973).

A history of the slave-naming tradition appears in Herbert George Gutman's *The Black Family in Slavery and Freedom, 1750–1925* (New York: Pantheon Books, 1976). Dan Rottenberg explains Jewish names in *Finding Our Fathers: A Guide to Jewish Genealogy* (New York: Random House, 1977). Jerome Anderson and Julie Helen Otto shared their information on the development of naming traditions in the United States.

American Given Names: Their Origin and History in the Context of the English Language (New York: Oxford University Press, 1979) is a good source for the meaning of personal names.

The history of Millis, Massachusetts, comes from *Place Names in Norfolk County, Massachusetts*, by Elmer O. Cappers (published for the County Historical Societies and Libraries, courtesy of Norfolk County Trust Co., n.d.), page 22. Place nicknames can be confusing until you consult *American Nicknames: Their Origin and Significance*, rev. ed., by George Earlie Shankle (New York: H. W. Wilson, 1955).

Chapter 5: Where to Find Help

An overview of the holdings of the Family History Library in Salt Lake City exists in Johni Cerny and Wendy Elliott's *The Library: A Guide to the LDS Family History*

Library (Salt Lake City: Ancestry, 1988).

A directory of genealogical libraries, archives, publishers, and organizations appears in Elizabeth Petty Bentley's *Genealogist's Address Book* (Baltimore: Genealogical Publishing, 1995).

Chapter 6: Helpful Technology

Three books help researchers negotiate the Web: Elizabeth Powell Crowe's *Genealogy Online: Researching Your Roots, Web Edition* (New York: Windcrest/McGraw-Hill, 1998); Cyndi Howell's *Netting Your Ancestors: Genealogical Research on the Internet* (Baltimore: Genealogical Publishing, 1997); and Laurie and Steve Bonner's *Searching for Cyber-Roots* (Salt Lake City: Ancestry, 1997).

Chapter 7: A Land of Many Cultures

Letters of Maria Little Kendall to her father in Vermont are in the personal collection of Lynn Betlock.

A good first-person account of life in Alaska is *A Schoolteacher in Old Alaska: The Story of Hannah Breece*, by Jane Jacobs (New York: Vintage Books, 1997). Advertisement from Minnesota taken from "Who Are Wanted in Minnesota," *St. Anthony Express*, June 21, 1851.

Additional information on U.S. passenger lists and where to find them appears in Michael Tepper's *American Passenger Arrival Records: A Guide to the Records of Immigrants Arriving at American Ports by Sail and Steam* (Baltimore: Genealogical Publishing, 1993). A series of volumes that indexes published passenger lists for the United States and Canada is *Passenger and Immigration Lists Index: A Guide to Published Arrival Records of 500,000 Passengers Who Came to the United States and Canada*, by P. William Filby and Mary K. Meyer (Detroit: Gale Research, 1981).

There are several useful guides to researching African American heritage. These include Donna Beasley's *Family Pride: The Complete Guide to Tracing African American Genealogy* (New York: Macmillan, 1997); Charles Blockson and Ron Fry's *Black Genealogy* (Baltimore: Black Classic Press, 1991); and David H. Street's *Slave Genealogy: A Research Guide with Case Studies* (Bowie, Md.: Heritage Books, 1986).

Two classic guides for Jewish genealogy are Arthur Kurzweil's *From Generation to Generation: How to Trace Your Jewish Genealogy and Family History* (New York: HarperCollins, 1994) and Dan Rottenberg's *Finding Our Fathers: A Guide to Jewish Genealogy* (New York: Random House, 1977).

For individuals tracing their Asian American heritage, a good reference book is Paula K. Byers's *Asian American Genealogical Sourcebook* (Detroit: Gale, 1995). For Hispanic American heritage, a good source is George Ryskamp's *Finding Your Hispanic Roots* (Baltimore: Genealogical Publishing, 1997).

A guide to reading documents in thirteen different languages is found in *Following the Paper Trail: A Bilingual Translation Guide* (Teaneck, N.J.: Avotaynu, 1994), by Jonathan D. Shea and William F. Hoffman.

Chapter 8: Wartime America

An excellent soldier's diary is Elisha Hunt Rhodes's *All for the Union* (New York: Random House, 1992). *Letters from an Iowa Soldier in the Civil War* can be found at www.ucsc.edu/civil-war-letters/scott_obit.html.

Mark H. Dunkleman's *Gettysburg's Unknown Soldier: The Life, Death, and Celebrity of Amos Humiston* (New York: Praeger, 1999 forthcoming) recounts the story of the Humiston children.

J. Albert Monroe's reminiscence is taken from *The Rhode Island Artillery at the First Battle of Bull Run* (Providence: Sidney S. Rider, 1878), 21. The story of the beans is the recollection of Ansel D. Nickerson, which appears in *A Raw Recruit's War Experiences* (Providence: Providence Press, 1888), 46–47. Samuel Downing and Alexander Milliner told their war stories in *Last Men of the Revolution,* by Reverend E. B. Hillard, edited by Wendell D. Garrett (Barre, Mass.: Barre Publishers, 1968), a reprint of the 1864 edition.

The advertisements for both John Brown and John Rynes appeared in the *Providence Gazette.* Sullivan Ballou's biography comes from *Brown University in the Civil War: A Memorial* (Providence: Brown University, 1868), 46–47.

Chapter 9: A Personal Story

Examples of illustrated family trees can be found in Peter Benes's "Decorated Family Records from Coastal Massachusetts, New Hampshire, and Connecticut" in *Families and Children, The Dublin Seminar for New England Folklife: Annual Proceedings 1985* (Boston: Boston University, 1985), 91–145.

A good history of handwriting is Tamara Plakins Thornton's *Handwriting in America: A Cultural History* (New Haven: Yale University Press, 1996).

Patricia Law Hatcher's *Producing a Quality Family History* (Salt Lake City: Ancestry, 1996) is a step-by-step guide to organizing and writing a genealogy. It is easy to understand and provides many examples of family histories.

An excellent set of books produced at the Westridge Young Writers Workshop in New Mexico includes *Kids Explore America's African American Heritage* (John Muir Publications, 1994); *Kids Explore America's Hispanic Heritage* (John Muir Publications, 1994); *Kids Explore America's Japanese American Heritage* (John Muir Publications, 1994); *Kids Explore America's Jewish Heritage* (John Muir Publications, 1994); and *Kids Explore the Heritage of Western Native Americans* (John Muir Publications, 1994). They were written by the children participating in the workshops. Each of the volumes in this series includes a history of the ethnic group, cultural information relating to holidays, and information on the language, as well as biographies of people in the community.

Chapter 10: Final Thoughts

For information on how to become a professional genealogist, see Sharon DeBartolo Carmack's *The Genealogy Source Book* (Los Angeles: Lowell House, 1997), 193–206.

Photo Credits

Front Matter: *p.i: Lynn Betlock; pp.ii-iii: Mark H. Dunkleman; p.viii left: All rights reserved. Charlotte Estey/Rhode Island Historical Society (RIHS) RHi(E791) 220; p.viii right: Grant Emison.*

Chapter 1: *p.x: George Tilley Wells/RIHS RHi(X3) 8829; p.2: Lynn Betlock; p.3: Casino Photo Studio/RIHS RHi(X3) 8836; p.4: Judy Gelles/Stock Boston.*

Chapter 2: *p.6: Grant Emison; p.8: RIHS RHi(X3) 2720; p.9: Grant Emison; p.10: RIHS RHi(X3) 8843; p.11: Grant Emison.*

Chapter 3: *p.14: Lynn Betlock; p.17 Courtesy of Genealogy Records Service. Forms available online at www.genrecords.com; p.19: Maureen Taylor; p.20: Courtesy of Genealogy Records Service; p.22 left: Lynn Betlock; p.22 right: Grant Emison; p.24: RIHS RHi(X3) 8833.*

Chapter 4: *p.26: Providence Journal-Bulletin photo; p.28: RIHS RHi(X3) 2818; p.31: RIHS RHi(X3) 6984; p.32: Missy Banis.*

Chapter 5: *p.36: Laima Druskis/Stock Boston; p.39: New England Historic Genealogical Society; p.41: RIHS RHi(X3) 8837; p.43: RIHS RHi(X3) 4334.*

Chapter 6: *p.44: Elizabeth Crews/Stock Boston; p.47: National Genealogical Society.*

Chapter 7: *p.50: Providence Journal-Bulletin photo; p.53: Grant Emison; p.55: RIHS RHi(X3) 879; p.56: Ansaldi Studios/RIHS RHi(X3) 8838; p.58: RIHS RHi(X3) 8841.*

Chapter 8: *p.60: RIHS RHi(X3) 714; p.63 left: Providence Journal-Bulletin photo; p.63 right: Frank Warren Marshall/RIHS RHi(X3) 1165; p.64: New York Historical Society; p.67: Mark H. Dunkleman; p.68: RIHS RHi(X3) 6402.*

Chapter 9: *p.70: Grant Emison; p.72 left: Grant Emison; p.72 right: RIHS RHi(X3) 6570; p.73: RIHS RHi(X3) 8840; p.74: NEHGS; p.75: RIHS RHi(X3) 8835.*

Chapter 10: *p.76: Lynn Betlock; p.78 left: RIHS RHi(X3) 8831; p.78 right: RIHS RHi(X3) 785; p.79: RIHS RHi(X3) 8839.*